AMERICAN INDIAN ART FROM THE DR. AND MRS. ROBERT B. PAMPLIN, JR. COLLECTION

KEEPING
THE
SPIRIT
ALIVE

OREGON HISTORICAL SOCIETY PRESS

PORTLAND, OREGON

BONNIE B. KAHN AND MARY D. SCHLICK

Oregon Historical Society
1200 SW Park
Portland, Oregon 97205

www.ohs.org

Designed and produced by the Oregon Historical Society Press.

We would like to extend our thanks to the photographers whose work appears in this book, Gary Eisley, Dennis Maxwell and Nayland Wilkins. Their initials are next to their work.

We would also like to thank the Maryhill Museum of Art in Goldendale, Washington for the use of their map "Regional Tribes & Trade Routes."

Library of Congress Cataloging-in-Publication Data
Kahn, Bonnie B.
        Keeping the spirit alive: American Indian art from the Dr. and Mrs. Robert B. Pamplin, Jr. collection/ Bonnie B. Kahn and Mary D. Schlick.
              p. cm.
        ISBN 0-87595-275-5
1. Indians of North America–material Culture–West(U.S.)–Catalogs. 2. Indian art–West (U.S.)–Catalogs. 3. Indians of North America–West (U.S.)–Antiquities–Catalogs. 4. West (U.S.)–Antiquities–catalogs. 5. Pamplin, Robert B., 1941–Enthonolgical collections–Catalogs. I. Title: American Indian art from the Dr. and Mrs. Robert B. Pamplin, Jr. Collection. II. Schlick, Mary Dodds. III. Oregon Historical Society. IV. Title.

E78.W5 K35 2001
978'.01'07479549--dc21

                                        2001016327

The paper used in this publication meets the minimum requirements of American National Standard for Information Sciences–Permanence of Paper for Printed Library Materials, ANSI Z39.48-1992.

TABLE OF CONTENTS

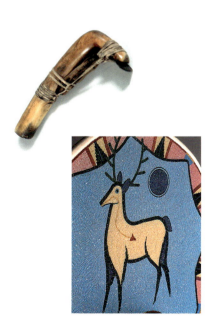

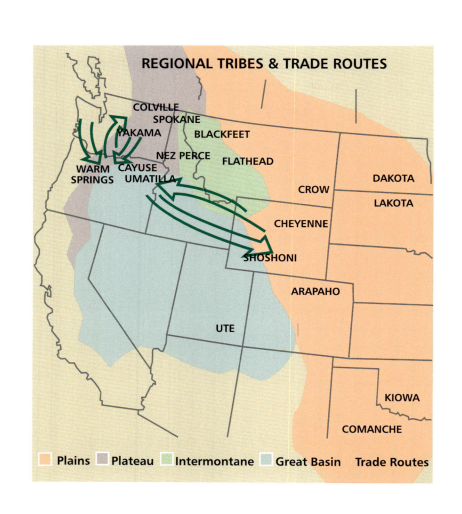

REGIONAL TRIBES & TRADE ROUTES

COLVILLE
SPOKANE
YAKAMA
BLACKFEET
NEZ PERCE
FLATHEAD
WARM CAYUSE
SPRINGS UMATILLA
DAKOTA
CROW
LAKOTA
CHEYENNE
SHOSHONI
ARAPAHO
UTE
KIOWA
COMANCHE

Plains   Plateau   Intermontane   Great Basin   Trade Routes

The collection of Dr. and Mrs. Robert B. Pamplin, Jr., spans a period of nearly 200 years of American Indian culture in the greater West. The focus of the collection is on those cultures — the Plains, Plateau, and some Great Basin tribes — that so readily adapted to the use of the horse. The inherent color, drama, and excitement of the visual imagery in the work of these groups first attracted Dr. Pamplin's attention. Over the years he developed a passion for these "things of great beauty" that has led to the creation of an outstanding collection ranging in breadth from the drama of the horse and war regalia to domestic objects of simple elegance. But the real importance of this collection is that it not only highlights and preserves the past, but also embraces the present and future by helping to conserve and preserve Native art forms. *Keeping the Spirit Alive* offers the public the opportunity to enjoy many beautiful objects from American Indian life through the generosity of Dr. and Mrs. Pamplin.

THE ARRIVAL OF THE HORSE IN the greater West early in the 1700s brought vast changes in the lives of the Native peoples of the Plains and the Columbia Plateau. When horses spread northward from Spanish settlements in the Southwest, they helped to expand Indian trade routes and hunting grounds, easing and enriching the lifestyles of various native groups. For some of the people of the Great Plains, the greater mobility led to an increase in warfare. Paintings on hides were the first records made by early warriors of these experiences on horseback.

D.M.

PLAINS INDIAN PAINTED BUFFALO HIDE ROBE, 1870s

Brain tanned buffalo hide, mineral pigments #1135

With the exception of rock art, among the oldest extant examples of Plains Indian drawings are those done on animal hides. Using a variety of pigments, early warriors recorded their coups and combats against other tribes as well as the United States cavalry on these hides. Lewis and Clark in their epic trip across the West collected a buffalo hide from the Mandan in 1805 showing an intertribal battle that took place in 1799.

Animal brains were used in the tanning process to give a velvety suppleness to the hide. Tanning in this manner and curing the hide with smoke kept the skin soft. It allowed wet hide to dry without stiffening.

Circling the robe in the Pamplin Collection are drawings of warriors, possibly Sioux fighting Crow. This robe is unusual in that the figures are circling the central sunburst motif, also referred to as the war bonnet motif. The drawings of horses' heads may be a way of telling how many horses were captured or killed.

In these robes, the action almost always flows from the right to the left unless there is an encounter and the warriors must turn to fight. Some believe this may be because a warrior mounted his horse on the right and carried his shield on his left arm. This robe was worn over and around the warrior's shoulders, hanging to the middle of his calf, overlapping in front with the portion that had been the buffalo's head to the wearer's left.

TELLING THE STORIES

AS THE LEDGER BOOKS used for accounting at Western forts became available to Native people through trade and other means, paper began to replace hide as the favored medium for recording important life events. The books were simpler to transport than buffalo robes and made it easy to share stories with companions.

Thirteen artists recorded their exploits in the Cheyenne/Arapaho Ledger Book from the Pamplin Collection. The ledger book dates back to the 1870's, with several pages reproduced here. Their drawings provide views of clothing and battle accouterments in use and demonstrate a love of ornament and beauty, even in wartime.

PLATE 15 OF CHEYENNE/ARAPAHO LEDGER BOOK

KIOWA NICKEL SILVER CROSS, 1870 or earlier

Hand tooled nickel silver, vermilion #1143

A cross-shaped pendant similar to the cross in the Pamplin Collection is proudly displayed upon a warrior's chest in Plate 15 of the Cheyenne/Arapaho Ledger Book. The crescent pendants from the cross resemble the *najas* seen on horse bridles and silver squash blossom necklaces made by silversmiths of the Southwest. The form derived from a Spanish saddlery decoration, which originated with the Moors in North Africa as a protection against the evil eye.

The term *naja* is from Navajo *najahe* meaning crescent. Such cres-cents are common decorations hung from cloud-shaped pectorals such as item#1020 on p. 11, and hung on crosses and headstalls from the mid-nineteenth century. Many Plains Indian men wore crosses of this type, perhaps purely as ornaments, but conceivably because they considered them to be imbued with symbolic meaning.

Note the complex rosette motif gracing the center of the cross and the profile of four males engraved on each arm, on the foot, and at the top of the cross. There is also evidence of vermilion pigment in parts of the engraving. The cross itself is cut from a rectangular sheet of nickel silver, an alloy of copper, nickel and zinc, approximately 2 mm. thick.

PLATE #172 FROM CHEYENNE/ARAPAHO LEDGER BOOK

SIOUX WARRIOR'S BREASTPLATE, 1890

Brain tanned deer hide, harness leather, glass trade beads and hairpipe bone beads #1023

The warrior in Plate #172 wears a breastplate. Made of beads fashioned from animal bone, long breastplates were popular items as adornment. Breastplates are often seen today at celebrations on the Plateau and Plains.

Long, tubular beads of conch shell were worn in the hair by eastern woodlands Indians in the early 1700s. Men would wear a single elongated hollow tube in their hair along either side of their face. This tube was called a hairpipe. By the late 19th century, cow bone imitations were being produced commercially by non-Indians in New England and notably, at the Armour Packing Company in Chicago. These were widely traded among the Plains tribes.

SOUTHERN PLAINS PECTORAL, 1860s

Nickel silver #1020

In Plate 172 a warrior wears a pectoral suspended from his hairpipe breastplate. Made of nickel silver, these ornaments have been popular among Cheyenne, Arapaho and other Plains men since the 1860s. The cloud-shaped ornament is rocker-engraved with three crescent-shaped pendants also referred to as naja.

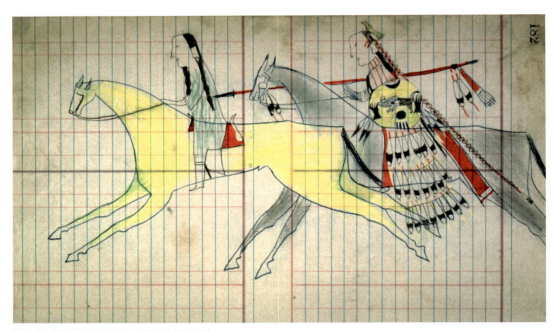

PLATE 182, FROM CHEYENNE/ARAPAHO LEDGER BOOK

**NICKEL SILVER HAIR PLATES,
1860s or earlier**

Nickel silver, trade cloth #1145

The warrior on the right in the
Cheyenne/Arapaho Ledger Book wears a set
of silver hair plates similar to this set in the
Pamplin Collection which have been
reassembled on red trade cloth for illustra-
tive purposes. Slightly domed, the plates
are rocker- engraved, and supplied with a
pair of triangular-shaped piercings for
mounting. Surviving sets of hairplates are
rare, although they remained popular with
southern Plains warriors through the end of
the 19th century.

WITH RECTO END PAPER B IN CHEYENNE/ARAPAHO LEDGER BOOK

ARAPAHO BLANKET STRIP ON TRADE BLANKET, 1870 – 1880

Trade cloth, buffalo hide, glass seed beads, sinew #1134

In Recto End Paper B, the decorative beaded strip worn by the mounted warrior is similar to the Arapaho blanket strip in the Pamplin Collection. Such decorative beaded strips were first attached to buffalo hides. The hides were split down the center during the tanning process then re-sewn with the beaded strips covering the seam. Trade cloth often replaced hides when it became available. The crosses at the shoulders (sometimes referred to as "butterflies") are recycled from an Arapaho moccasin toe. Instead of hemming the undyed selvedge on the trade cloth, Plains Indian people used it as part of the decoration.

D.M.

PLATE #168 OF CHEYENNE/ARAPAHO LEDGER BOOK

SIOUX BOW CASE, 1870s

Buffalo hide, porcupine quills, and glass seed beads #1036

In Plate #168 of the ledger, a Pawnee warrior (identified by his distinctive cuff-like moccasins) wears a bow case over his shoulder similar to the Sioux bow case in the Pamplin Collection.

Constructed of brain-tanned buffalo hide and ornamented with dyed porcupine quills and glass seed beads, this quiver-bow case is an example of warrior equipment used during the Indian Wars Period of the 1870s. The neat and narrow lanes of quillwork are a distinctive Sioux decoration of quiver-bow cases during this period.

ARAPAHO MOCCASINS, Circa 1870

Buffalo hide, glass seed beads and sinew #1094

A pair of Arapaho moccasins nearly identical in design to the pair in the Pamplin Collection is shown in the Cheyenne/Arapaho Ledger Book, Plate 212 Made of buffalo hide, with buffalo rawhide soles and sewn with sinew, these are representative of those produced during the era of the last buffalo hunts in the 1870s. Few moccasins from this period survive as most were worn out, recycled or discarded.

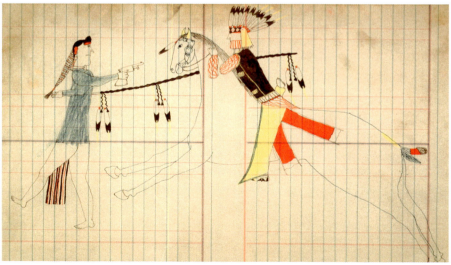

PLATE 212 OF CHEYENNE/ARAPAHO LEDGER BOOK

PLATE YZ REVERSE IN CHEYENNE/ ARAPAHO LEDGER BOOK

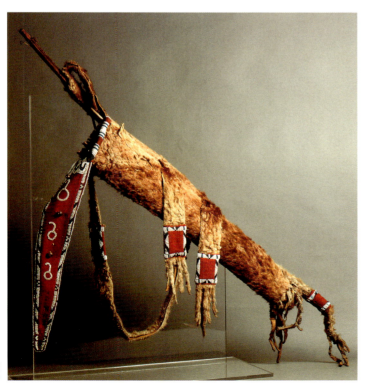

KIOWA OR KIOWA/APACHE OTTERSKIN BOW CASE AND QUIVER, Circa 1860

Otterskin, trade cloth, brass bells, glass seed beads, sinew. Bow is wooden and sinew backed #1096

The ledger shows a Cheyenne warrior bravely riding his horse through a hail of bullets with his highly prized otter skin bow case and quiver at his side.

On looking at this case, Bill Holm, curator emeritus of the University of Washington's Burke Museum, made the following comments: "Otter skin was one of the favorite animal skins for American Indians because it was so luxurious. For this bow case, the entire otter skin was used. The tab of the bow case was created from the tail of the otter. The wooden bow is wrapped in sinew, which made the arrow travel faster. For a warrior, it was brave to carry an elaborate bow case into battle. It drew attention and you became a target to the enemy who may want to steal the bow case from you."

YANKTONAI SIOUX RIFLE SCABBARD, 1870–1880

Buffalo and deer hide, glass trade beads, variety of pigments, and sinew #1035

When Plains peoples acquired firearms, they decorated the new cases just as they had the cases for bows and arrows. This scabbard is made of brain-tanned buffalo and deer hide, the strap recycled from a buffalo robe.

LAKOTA SIOUX KNIFE BLADE CLUB, 1870s

Three blades marked J. Russell 1872. Oak, brass tacks, iron nails, vermilion pigment #1093

Early warriors adapted weaponry to the horse, such as this knife blade club. Its great length enabled a rider to hold the club and swing it to attack his enemy. Such clubs were highly prized by Sioux men, and few survive.

This club is an excellent example of adapting a foreign technology for individual needs. The three blades stamped "J. Russell 1872" were manufactured by John Russell's factory during the five year span, 1868 to 1873, when his factory was in Turner's Falls, Massachusetts. Russell knives were considered among the top blades manufactured in the United States at that time. Set in an oak handle, these blades made the club an especially lethal weapon. The tacks decorating the handle are Brummagen cast brass from Birmingham, England shipped to the United States between 1840 and 1860. The wood was polished with a type of ground pumice in use before power tools. Vermilion pigment was rubbed into the handle and a light burning added as a form of ornamentation.

PLAINS SPONTOON PIPE TOMAHAWK, 1860–1880

Steel, ash wood #1033

Pipe tomahawks could be smoked or used in combat. Decorated by hot file branding, they were popular trade items on the Plains and Plateau. Although once used as a weapon, because of the time period of this pipe tomahawk, it was more likely used as a trade item or for smoking. The blade was hand forged from blister steel, the most common basic steel before the Bessemer process was perfected during the Civil War period. The surface of the blade was case hardened, which was the phrase used by 19th century metalworkers meaning "to harden on the outside."

PLAINS CREE KNIFE SHEATH, Circa 1870s

Hide, glass seed beads, tin, leather, porcupine quills #1040

Sheaths that cover and preserve knives were often worn attached to a belt to make them more easily accessible. The abstract beadwork style, quill-wrapped fringe and tin cones identify this sheath as the work of the Plains Cree or their Chipewyan neighbors in the north. The maker has recycled some of the beadwork from an earlier case.

PLAINS QUIRT, Circa 1860

Elk horn and harness leather #1075

The act of touching a living enemy in battle and safely escaping exposed the warrior to the greatest danger and was the most highly acclaimed of all "coups." Plains warriors used quirts to count coup in battle as well as to goad their horses. Quirts made from the long tines of an elk antler, the surface smoothed and polished to a high gloss, were highly prized on the Plains. This example was carried across the Great Plains from Council Bluffs, Iowa.

CROW TACKED KNIFE SHEATH, late 19th century

Harness leather, brass tacks #1125

Knife cases of harness leather decorated by brass tacks were popular with Plains and Plateau men. Harness leather was often recycled from worn out saddles and other types of horsegear. Brass tacks were a trade commodity used to decorate lances, guns, tomahawks, knife blade clubs and many other items.

CELEBRATION

THE HORSE MADE GREATER CONTACT among Native groups possible. This inspired elaborate ornamentation for the people of the Plains and Plateau and their mounts. By the early 19th century, a traveler to the West found the Native people "fond of fine dresses . . . and gay trappings for their horses." Early journal accounts mentioned people and horses "gaily accoutered" and "richly and gorgeously dressed."

It was common for prominent men to own more than a thousand horses. Crow horse equipment was some of the most elaborately beaded on the Plains, reaching its most showy stage between 1880 and 1910.

Horses had been traded into the Plateau region in the early 1700s and became very important to Plateau people who continue today to decorate both the rider and the horse for parades held at annual encampments and celebrations.

The Native peoples' love of beauty and ornamentation is alive to this day. It is demonstrated all year long across North America at large celebrations and powwows, at fairs, and on longhouse ceremonial occasions. As you turn these pages, try to imagine yourself joining in the traditional gatherings.

CROW MARTINGALE, 1870–1910

Trade cloth, cotton ticking, calico, hide, glass seed beads, brass bells #1063

Martingales were seen on both men's and women's horses on the Plains and Plateau, a tradition continuing today. This Crow martingale can be seen in the photograph to the right, taken between 1910 and 1916. In this photograph, a proud Crow father named Grasshopper holds the reins to a horse ridden by his small daughter. The martingale hangs from the horse's neck.

CIRCLE TIME ON THE COLVILLE RESERVATION

MAKE YOUR WAY THROUGH the dry grass onto the Circle grounds south of Nespelem, Washington. People are all about, but the only sound is the rhythmic cadence of horses walking, and bells.

Someone whispers, "There's his horse." You see the empty saddle, placed backwards on the horse, with stirrups swinging gently, and you remember that this Fourth of July celebration on the Colville reservation is held in memory of a Nez Perce leader who recently died. This is his horse, and his empty saddle.

The pace quickens; the memorial circle completed, the riders and their mounts are on parade. You notice the finery, much like the bright beaded martingales, the painted crupper, the rare mountain lion saddle throw, and the woven horse drape decorated with flying birds that surround you in this exhibit.

A horse wears a beaded floral band across its chest. A young woman astride another horse holds a folded blanket decorated with a beaded blanket strip across her lap; a big star-design twined storage bag hangs from her saddle. Another rider sits astride a rare woman's saddle with matching stirrups, saddle throw, and bridle. The procession is a moving display of family heirlooms.

GRASSHOPPER AND HIS DAUGHTER (COURTESY DEPT. OF LIBRARY SERVICES, AMERICAN MUSEUM OF NATURAL HISTORY, #118959)

"Items were decorated not only to show the wealth of the owner but also because it made them pleasing to the eye."

Daryel Lopez

D.M.

COLVILLE INDIAN WOMEN AT 1955 FOURTH OF JULY ENCAMPMENT. PHOTO BY W.T. SCHLICK.

NEZ PERCE MARTINGALE, Circa 1900.

Cloth, ermine, glass seed beads, mirrors #1141

Martingales were often passed down through generations. This particular martingale appeals to many of the senses. The bells gently ring as the martingale sways with the movement of the horse, the mirrors reflect the light, and the beads and ermine add to the visual and textural appeal of the martingale. The floral pattern became popular on Plateau martingales after 1900.

*Italicized quotations are from the video The Pamplin Collection of Art. It is noted in the Sources section.

"A bird, such as an eagle, was a messenger who took our prayers to the heavens. Smaller birds were guides to help people who were lost at night and did not have the aid of the moon."

Maynard White Owl Lavadour

PLATEAU HORSE DRAPE, 19th to 20th century

Cornhusk, buckskin and wool #1109

This unusual horse drape is decorated with matching panels of twining with false embroidery, a basketry technique. The drape is usually hung across the rump of the horse behind the saddle and sometimes had pockets sewn at either end that could be stuffed with goods. The long fringes served two purposes: they demonstrated the prowess of the hunter who killed the animal for the hide and they were beautiful as they swayed with the movement of the horse.

CIRCLE TIME ON THE COLVILLE RESERVATION

"I remember stories my great grandmother told me of her grand-mother carving this style of saddle out of green cottonwood using only a large butcher knife as a tool."

Maynard White Owl Lavadour

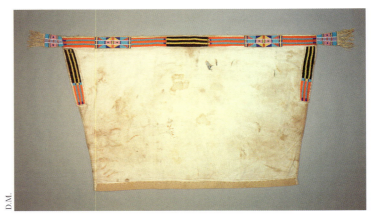

CROW HORSE ENSEMBLE, 1870–1920

Leather, wood, cotton and trade cloth, glass seed beads, pigments, horsehair #1065, 1066, 1067

This saddle, saddle blanket and horsehair bridle are typical of what would be owned by a Crow family. This style of wooden-frame was adapted by the Crow, Nez Perce, and Shoshone from the Spanish saddle, the high pommel and cantle in front distinguishing it as a woman's saddle.

Beaded decorations in a style typical of the Crow during this period are sewn to a blanket made from flour sacks and woolen trade cloth.

The stirrups are painted rawhide. Both saddle and stirrups are further embellished with beadwork. For the bridle, a recycled parfleche container may have been used along with horsehair and beads. According to some of the Plateau tribes, the keyhole motif on the front of the bridle is said to reflect the circular shape of a corral with the funnel opening for the horses.

D.M.

NEZ PERCE CHEST ORNAMENT. circa 1895–1905

Trade cloth, glass seed beads, leather, tin cone tinklers #1031

Tin cone tinklers attached to this band with its classic beaded floral design add motion when tied across the horse's chest in a parade. Originally cut from metal tobacco box lids, other metal containers or sheet metal, these cones became popular ornamentation on Native regalia.

G.E.

D.M.

CROW MOUNTAIN LION SADDLE DRAPE, Mid to late 19th century

Mountain lion skin and trade cloth #1064

In pre-contact times, furs such as mountain lion and wolf were used as cushions between the saddle and the horse. During the late Indian Wars Period in the 19th century, we see more use of the trade blanket for this purpose. Mountain lion skins, lined with red trade cloth, were highly prized saddle throws for Plains warriors from at least the 1830s. Display of the skin meant the warrior was a good hunter. They have also been used on the Plateau for men's saddle blankets, according to Maynard White Owl Lavadour, Cayuse/Nez Perce artist.

NEZ PERCE CRUPPER, Late 19th century with 20th century repairs

Rawhide, pigments, glass seed beads, trade cloth #1068

This painted rawhide crupper, decorated with beaded panels, goes under the tail of the horse and connects by straps to the saddle, holding it in place.

"The hour glass figure in the blanket strip stands for a woman and the hourglass with a square stands for a man. When a man and woman would marry they would stand in the middle of a floor with a blanket such as this during a wedding....."

Maynard White Owl Lavadour

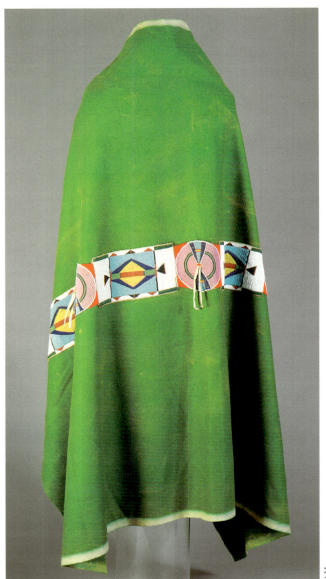

CROW BLANKET STRIP ON TRADE BLANKET, 1870–1880

Trade cloth, buffalo hide sinew, porcupine quills, and glass seed beads #1002

The beadwork is stitched on buffalo hide with sinew and then attached to green wool trade cloth, identified by its undyed selvedge. The rosettes on the strip are made of porcupine quill-wrapped rings with red woolen centers.

YAKAMA STORAGE BAG, Late 19th century

Spun dogbane, cornhusk, wool yarn #1077

The different designs on the two sides of this bag are examples of the symmetry and rhythmic repetition of motifs that characterize the large flat bags of the Plateau. Twined with spun dogbane and, in recent times, cotton or linen warps and wefts, they usually are covered with cornhusk and/or yarn false embroidery. False embroidery, also known as external weft wrap, is a weaving technique in which a flat strand such as cornhusk or grass is wrapped around the outside weft. This covering cannot be seen on the inside of the bag. Such weaves are tight and dust-proof and the dogbane makes them insect-resistant.

A VISIT TO A TEPEE

You stroll through the Circle grounds looking for the tepee of the Colville Indian Agency groundskeeper. He has asked you to stop by after the parade. Just as you are wondering how to knock at a tepee, he and his wife call from within and invite you to enter. You step inside. Soft sunlight filters through the white canvas, and you see heirlooms hanging from a clothesline stretched between the tepee poles.

Your host and his wife tell you the history of each object as you admire it at close range. You marvel at the beadwork and fine basketry passed down through their Umatilla and Yakama families and at the beautiful gifts presented to them on visits to other tribes.

CAYUSE WOMAN'S HANDBAG, Circa 1900

Dogbane or cotton, cornhusk, aniline dye #1133

Large twined flat cornhusk bags were used for storage and the smaller ones were used as handbags. This bag is a rarity because it has the same design motifs on both sides and the background is dyed rather than in the natural color of the cornhusk. On the opposite side, the design is in purple and yellow, with the same background color.

OJIBWA/CREE COAT, Circa 1870s

Caribou hide, beaver fur, glass seed beads #1010

The style of this beaded, caribou hide coat trimmed in beaver is based on European models. Photos of Plateau and Crow men taken around 1900 show tribal leaders wearing coats similar to this. Some scholars cite European fabrics and embroidery as the inspiration for the floral motifs, however, many Native beadworkers say they are inspired by the flowers around them.

TLINGIT OCTOPUS BAG, 19th century

Trade cloth, glass seed beads, wool yarn #1126

Many of these men's bags made their way onto the Plateau with the fur trade. The name comes from the distinctive eight tabs, four on each side. Worn hanging from a wide, decorated strap that crossed the chest, these bags were used for carrying personal items. Yarn tassels are frequently seen on Tlingit bags, which usually are beaded in leaflike scroll shapes.

TLINGIT OR TAHLTAN CARTRIDGE BELT, 1870s

Trade cloth, glass seed beads, metal liners #1042

Tied around the waist, the cartridge belt made ammunition for firepower more accessible. The stylized floral beading style also appears on knife cases from the North. The belts were traded across the Plains. The metal liners were used to hold rifle cartridges.

SANTEE SIOUX DOUBLE-SIDED POUCH, Circa 1885

Hide, glass seed beads, cloth #1048

Glass seed beads, available by the mid 1800s, allowed beadworkers to express themselves in new ways. This beautiful circular beaded bag with American flag motifs on one side may have been made for trade or as a prized item for a man or woman to carry for celebrations.

D.M.

SIOUX BUFFALO HIDE MOCCASINS, 1870–880

Buffalo hide, glass seed beads, sinew thread #1009

Affluent Plains Indians displayed their wealth by beading the moccasin soles as well as the tops and wore this type of moccasin for special occasions. The beads were sewn onto the hide using sinew, the strong strands of the tendon that runs along either side of an animal's backbone.

LAKOTA COW HIDE ROBE, 1880 or earlier

Cow hide, horse hair, dentalium shells, porcupine quills, dyed chicken feathers #1140

Embellished with porcupine quills (restored) and dentalium shells with horsehair, this elegant robe shows hours of careful work. In time, the use of glass seed beads replaced much of this age-old tradition of working with quills. This robe would have been worn by a woman for special occasions. In his classic work on porcupine quill decoration, William Orchard mentions that hunting porcupine often fell to the men and that they sometimes plucked the quills from a living animal. Quills taken from the tail were large and coarse and were used in broad masses of embroidery. The finest quills came from the belly and were used for the most delicate lines.

D.M.

WOMEN'S DANCE CONTEST - YAKAMA

PARADES ARE SPECTACLES IN MOTION, but indoor celebrations offer a closer look at the finery worn on special occasions. Imagine that you are invited to judge a women's dance contest at the pavilion near Toppenish Creek Longhouse on the Yakama reservation.

As the drummers seated around the huge drum begin their insistent beat, quiet at first then steadily louder, you stand with the other judge in the center of the pavilion and watch beautifully dressed contestants step gracefully around the floor. The master of ceremonies tells you the choice is up to you. "You're the judges," he says. The women move sedately, eyes cast down, necklaces and fringes on their dresses swinging in rhythm to the drum.

They circle past you again and again until the drumming stops. The master of ceremonies, the onlookers, and the women standing side by side look at you expectantly, but you are no closer to a decision than when the song began. You both feel this decision is important; it could set the tone of your welcome among the Yakama over many years to come. You ask for another song, then a third.

At last you agree on first-, second-, and third-place winners. The audience bursts into laughter and applause. Somehow you have passed the test. By chance, you have chosen the wife of the tribal chairman, the daughter of a well-recognized traditionalist, and a much-loved visitor from a nearby reservation.

YAKAMA DRESS, 1890–1920

Glass beads, dentalium shells, trade cloth #1005

This dress of navy blue trade cloth is ornamented with glass beads and hundreds of dentalium shells. Scholar Stephen Grafe points out that in an 1846 letter to his friend Dudley Allen, Henry Spalding (a missionary to the Nez Perce) described a dress similar to the one displayed. "The Aquois [dentalium shells] are very costly....shells from a single dress were once taken to the mountains by a man who lives near, & sold in small parcels for $1,600.00."

In the same letter, he mentioned that "A young lady...in one of these dresses, upon a firey horse well equipped with saddle & crouper, makes a fine appearance." The market value in 2000 of the $1,600 Henry Spalding mentions would be $32,000.

N.W.

D.M.

BLACKFEET PANEL BELT, 1890

Harness leather, glass seed beads, brass tacks, sinew, leather thongs #1101

The pink beads, which are strung with sinew thread, appear uneven when the belt is flat, when worn around the waist, the beads tighten and the design becomes even. This style of panel belt continues to be in use across the Plains and Plateau.

NEZ PERCE FOLDOVER PURSE, 1920

String, cornhusk, wool yarn, fabric, hide thong, glass seed beads, trade beads #1076

Usually worn on a belt, these purses are made by twining with false embroidery. They feature three surfaces, the pocket front, pocket back, and the flap, each decorated in a different design. The beaded edge is an especially fine finish for this bag.

D.M.

**PLAINS OR PLATEAU BANDOLIER
NECKLACE, late 19th century**

**Hairpipe bone beads, shells, and blue
faceted glass beads #1025**

The name, "bandolier" refers to the wide
cartridge strap worn diagonally across the
chest by soldiers and later adapted in many
parts of the world for ceremonial dress.
This necklace style, worn by both Native
men and women for festive occasions, has
been given the bandolier name for it's simi-
larity in shape to those straps.

D.M.

31

GRAND ENTRY AT WARM SPRINGS

EACH YEAR IN LATE JUNE you try not to miss the Grand Entry at the Pi-ume-sha celebration on the Warm Springs reservation. Just after noon on a sunny Saturday, men, women, and children wearing their best ceremonial outfits follow the flag bearers into the grassy arena. Hearing the deep heartbeat of the big drum, you climb into the bleachers that surround the green and stand at attention with other onlookers, hand over your heart as the flags enter, glad to be part of this day.

Men in military uniforms or full warrior regalia lead the procession, stepping in time to the drumming, flags held high. The men dancers follow, stately in headdresses of eagle feathers, buffalo horn or cougar. You admire the heirloom bandolier bags and hairpipe breastplates. Some of the men hold beaded or woven pouches; some wear rare arm bands woven in the old way, or decorated breast-plates. The dancers are dressed in the regalia and the style of moccasin distinctive to their home territories.

HEADDRESS Maynard White Owl Lavadour, Cayuse/Nez Perce, 1998.

Buckskin, turkey feathers, moosehide, hair locks, trade cloth, glass seed beads, wool yarn, ochre #3003

Seven dozen feathers fall from a moose hide cap decorated with red dots of ochre to form a double trailer headdress. While eagle feathers and white ermine were used in constructing traditional headpieces in bygone years, this headdress was made from hand-painted turkey feathers, a common custom among Native people today.

The headdress is shown with a back view of the war shirt pictured on the opposite page.

"Smoking darkened the hides, preserved them and kept them soft, and kept [moccasins] from getting ruined when it became damp."

Maynard White Owl Lavadour

D.M.

PLATEAU MEN'S CUFFED MOCCASINS, Circa 1870

Buffalo hide, sinew, and glass seed beads #1097

Although both men and women on the Plateau wore moccasins with floral patterns, this particular pair was made for a man during the era of the last buffalo hunts in the 1870s. Women's moccasins would have a higher wrap around the leg or would be worn with leggings.

WAR SHIRT [front view] Maynard White Owl Lavadour, Cayuse/Nez Perce 1998.

Recipient of Oregon Governor's Arts Award 1997

Buckskin, hair locks, trade cloth, glass seed beads, wool yarn, ochre #3002

Maynard White Owl Lavadour has constructed this man's traditional war shirt from three white tanned deer hides. He has used natural ocher pigment to create solid red dots, which in earlier times would represent an enemy's life taken. The red yarn-wrapped bundles of human hair (in this instance, from a beauty salon) represent the spirit or power taken from the enemy. The motif formed by the red and dark blue wool on the front and back bibs is said to represent grizzly bear paws for strength. Coups earned by touching an enemy in battle are signified by hand marks on the shirt.

D.M.

"This headdress would have been worn by men who were Indian doctors or who had received something very strong and powerful during their vision quest."

Maynard White Owl Lavadour

D.M.

CROW BUFFALO HORN HEADDRESS, Circa 1890–1910

Ermine pelt, cotton canvas, leather, buffalo horns, and beads #1013

A set of buffalo horns adorns this magnificent headdress set with a full crown of ermine pelts sewn to a cotton canvas cap with similar pelts draping the neck. Such headdresses were popular among men of the Northern Plains and Plateau regions.

D.M.

CROW COUGAR HEADDRESS, Circa 1870 or earlier

Cougar skin, brass tacks, trade cloth #1100

Headdresses of the entire skin of a cougar or mountain lion's head are an ancient and widely distributed type of headpiece, found from the Navajo in the southwest to the Cree in Canada. Although descriptions of these headdresses exist and appear in some historic photographs, very few survived. This fine example, collected from the Crow decades ago, is one of the few extant headdresses of its type to have survived the Indian Wars of the 1860s-1870s.

The ears on this rare head covering are formed from leather; brass tacks accentuate the eyes. The tacks are Brummagen cast brass circa 1840 and have been scratched with a fine chisel to accentuate the eye area.

HARLISH WASHSHOMAKE OR CHIEF WOLF NECKLACE AND HIS INTERPRETER. (SMITHSONIAN INSTITUTION, NEG. 55685)

TWINED PLATEAU POUCH, Circa 1900

Cotton twine, cornhusk, wool yarn #1117

Plateau men often carried small bags as part of ceremonial dress. In 1894, Harlish Washshomake, also known as Palouse Chief Wolf Necklace, posed for a formal portrait in Washington, D.C. holding a similar round pouch with spiral design woven with cornhusk false embroidery.

NEZ PERCE MAN'S ARMBANDS, 1870s

String, cornhusk, cotton fabric and wool yarn #1106

Although the twined root storage bags of the Plateau are the most common uses of this distinctive cornhusk false embroidery basketry technique, vests and other articles of men's dress occasionally were made in this way. These Nez Perce armbands at one time belonged to a Montana Salish chief.

N.W.

D.M.

UTE TAIL BAG, 1880–1890

Beads, tanned hide, glass seed beads, brass button #1111

Once owned by a Ute chief, this bag is a fine example of Ute beadwork. The strictly decorative tail at the bottom of the bag is used primarily by the Ute and Jicarilla Apache, and to a limited extent, by the Arapaho.

D.M.

SIOUX MAN'S BREASTPLATE, Circa 1900

Cowhide, porcupine quills, rawhide, tin cones, dyed chicken feathers and mirrors #1144

This breastplate is an example of the wide variety of trade items used by the Sioux. The mirrors in graduated sizes were especially popular items brought by traders, and can be seen today at powwows across the continent at the center of some fancy dancers' feather bustles. This piece was once owned by actor/writer Will Rogers.

UMATILLA MAN'S BANDOLIER BAG, 1850–1890

Buffalo hide, trade cloth, brass buttons, pony beads, glass seed beads, sinew #1057

These bags were worn over the shoulder and across the chest to hold personal belongings and for ceremonial wear. Similar bags also served as martingales for horses. Brass Brummagen buttons combine with pony beads to embellish this bag of beaded hide and trade cloth.

Pony bead is a collector's term for small round glass beads that were originally retailed as "pound beads" during the fur trade period in western North America, ca. 1790-1850. Fine bags of this type first appear in photographs of Ute men during the 1860s and 1870s. By the late 19th and early 20th century these bags are also seen in photographs of Plateau men. This bag, with beadwork entirely composed of the earlier pound beads (later replaced by smaller glass seed beads), must have been produced prior to 1880. The red cloth tabs which overlay the red cloth panel at the bottom of the bag recall the tassels found on the sleeves and hoods of blanket coats known as capotes (see p. 53.) made by the Nez Perce and their neighbors. Although the exact tribal affiliation of this bag is unknown, it is one of the finest and earliest examples of its type extant.

Maynard White Owl Lavadour tells a Cayuse story about a chief who fought a grizzly bear. When the chief finally won the battle and the bear died, the man accepted the animal's spirit, becoming powerful like the bear. Taking pride in the scars across his chest made by the bear, he wore red claw marks on the strap of his bandolier bag to commemorate the battle.

NEXT COME THE WOMEN, regal as they step to the tempo of the powwow drum. An amazing hat catches the light. The brimless shape is traditional, but the hat's surface is covered with a bird and floral scene worked in tiny cut seed beads. Plateau women have used basketry techniques to weave such hats since earliest times. Today's artists use beadwork to stretch their designing skills beyond the traditional geometric motifs.

A small Arapaho girl, proud in her heirloom dress and small concho belt, hurries to keep up with her mother, who steps out in fully beaded moccasins and high leggings. Eyes turn to a woman in an elegant cape completely covered in dentalium shells and edged with brass beads that swing on black beaded fringe.

ARAPAHO CHILD'S DRESS
19th century

Buckskin, mescal beads, tin cones #1152

Fringes, mescal beads and tin cone tinklers—all would be in motion when a small girl wore this handsewn buckskin dress. The beads are seeds from beans of the mescal plant, *Sophora secundiflora*, an evergreen shrub found primarily in parts of Texas, southern New Mexico, and Mexico. The beans were traded by Indian people living in these regions to tribes on the Southern Plains. Such silver concho belts, made of discs of sterling silver on harness leather, were popular adornment for men, women, and children.

BEADED PLATEAU STYLE WOMAN'S HAT
Doris Shippentower, Yakama/Umatilla/Navajo, 1998.

Cloth, glass seed beads, 24-carat gold beads #3004

On this hat, made in the traditional shape of ancient Plateau basketry hats, the fine beadwork depicts hummingbirds aflutter within blooming trumpet vines. By using her maiden name, the award-winning artist gives credit to her mother, the late Hazel Shippentower, for all the encouragement given to her. Her Umatilla grandmother, Yew-Nat-Pum, also was well known for her fine beadwork.

ARAPAHO WOMEN'S HIGH-TOP MOCCASINS, pre-1889

Hide, sinew, glass seed beads, nickel silver #1148

These Arapaho boot moccasins are decorated with nickel silver conchos and lanes of lazy stitch beadwork in distinctly Arapaho patterns. While moccasins and knee-high leggings were worn by Plains women, it was only on the Southern Plains and among the neighboring Ute that they were combined into a one-piece boot. Cheyenne and Arapaho women's boot moccasins differ from those of other Southern Plains tribes in using considerably more beadwork (with distinctive patterns), a slightly different shape of the moccasin sole and different cut of the moccasin upper.

"In the old days, women were not allowed to speak at certain cere-monies. Yet, what they wore and sometimes how elaborate the item was, would identify to others how wealthy her family was.

Sophie George

N.W.

SIOUX DENTALIUM SHELL CAPE, 1880—1910

Dentalium shells, brass and glass beads, ribbon, cording, hide, fabric.

This beautiful garment would be worn as a yoke over a woman's buckskin, trade cloth, or velvet dress for tribal celebrations across the continent, the brass bead-edged fringes swinging with the dancer's graceful steps.

Native people originally gathered valuable tusk-shaped dentalium shells off the Pacific Coast from Vancouver Island to Sitka, Alaska. Used as a medium of exchange, some shells were traded inland as far as the Southern Plains. Scholar Robert Stearns wrote in 1889 that with the arrival of the Europeans, a form of dentalium which is abundant in the Atlantic Ocean and obtained in Europe was imported for the Indian trade. This dentalium is nearly identical in appearance to that from the Pacific Northwest, and it is these European shells which were used to decorate this Sioux cape. Wool cloth, the backing for the shells on this garment, was the standard material for making such a cape in the late 19th century when dentalium shell dresses and yokes became popular among Sioux women. It replaced the heavier antelope or deer hide for native clothing.

CELEBRATIONS SUCH AS THE Circle at Nespelem or Pi-ume-sha at Warm Spings or the Speelyi-Mi Arts and Crafts Fair on the Yakama reservation are not performances for entertainment, although onlookers are welcome. They are occasions for bringing out treasured keepsakes, and they are joyous opportunities to gather with relatives and friends to have a good time, keeping the spirit alive.

LEONARD TOMASKIN, WATSON AND TILLIE TOTUS WITH THE TOTUS DISPLAY AT SPEELYI-MI ARTS AND CRAFTS FAIR, WAPATO, WASHINGTON. PHOTO BY MARY SCHLICK.

TREASURES FOR TYGH VALLEY

THE COUNTY AGENT'S TRUCK CLIMBS the hill above Warm Springs Agency and stops at the house of a tribal elder. The agent is on his way to the Wasco County Fair. When he goes to the door, the elder asks him to carry a big metal suitcase to the truck. There on the tailgate she opens the lid.

Inside are twined bags, beadwork, and many other beautiful things usually seen only in museums. The county agent will carry these keepsakes over the hills to the fairgrounds nestled at the foot of the mountains west of Tygh Valley.

The elder will come later to set up her booth beside those of other Warm Springs families who have taken part in this fair for many years. Each booth is a mini-museum. When the exhibitor is present, the exhibit labeling is spoken and personal.

You visit the fair and walk in wonderment from booth to booth. Reservation families often display prized personal keepsakes at local fairs. Especially rare items on view today are a man's toilet kit of brush, comb, tweezers, razor, and mirror, all carried in a beaded pouch; a great-grandmother's hide scraper and chokecherry pounding tools; a fine wallet made by a weaver from the Tillamook people, at the mouth of the Columbia River.

Elaborate dentalium adornments have been passed down through generations. The hard-to-gather shells from the Northwest Coast represent great wealth. Chinese coins, cobalt blue beads, and the white heart Cornaline d'Aleppo beads all add to the worth of these dentalium articles to the Native people.

The designs and carvings on the early Wasco/Wishxam pieces show their close connection to the natural world.

CHEYENNE TOILET KIT, late 1890s century

Recycled leather and glass seed beads #1112

This bag, recycled from the two sides panels of a storage bag known as a "possible" bag. The name comes from the Sioux term translated as a bag for every possible thing. It contains a rare collection of personal items for a man's use: a cowhorn comb, porcupine brush, metal tweezers, mirror, and a metal razor. The mixture of native and non-native toilet items was common on the Plains in the late 19th century.

LAKOTA SIOUX BERRY POUNDING KIT AND ASSINIBOINE CHERRY POUNDER, 1900 or earlier

Stone, rawhide, wood. #1105

Once necessary food preparation equipment for a woman of the Plains, these pounding kits are among the few that survive today.

TILLAMOOK WALLET, 1800–1840

Cattail, bear grass, cedar bark #1077A

Trade was common into the Plateau from the mouth of the Columbia River for coast tribes such as the Tillamook. Woven of cattail with beargrass and cedar bark overlay, this early example of Tillamook weaving portrays the horned grebe known as "helldiver" among Pacific Coastal weavers. The vertical lines in the other design are known as "hands" or "fingers."

PLAINS HIDE SCRAPER, 1900 or earlier

Bone, leather, iron, #1103

The iron blade is recycled from an 1860s gun and hand sharpened. Design patterns along the sides and top of the scraper were burned in with a type of metal awl, possibly to prevent the hand from slipping when using it as a tool or to hold the rawhide binding in place. The marks may also have served as a personal record for the woman who used the scraper. Colonel Richard Irving Dodge described the use of the hide-scraper this way: "When the stretched skin [of the animal] has become dry and hard from the action of the sun, the woman goes to work upon it with a small implement, shaped somewhat like a carpenter's adze. It has a short handle of wood or elkhorn, tied on with rawhide, and is used with one hand. These tools are heirlooms in families, and greatly prized. It is exceeding difficult to obtain one, especially one with an elk-horn handle, the Indians valuing them above price."

WASCO/WISHXAM BAG, Circa 1880

Dogbane (Apocynum cannibinum) and tule (Scirpus acutus) #1127

Wasco weavers and their Wishxam neighbors across the Columbia River developed a distinctive stylized human figure said to represent "the old ones," possibly referring to ancestors. It has been suggested that there is a relationship between the basketry designs of these Upper Chinookan weavers and the distinctive rock art found in the Columbia Gorge. On the reverse side of the bag are two columns of sturgeon figures, the main food of the Wasco/Wishxam people.

"Highly valued trade items, the horns of the bighorn sheep become extremely flexible when heated with boiling water. The incising of the bowls required tremendous effort; even with contemporary tools it is extremely difficult."

Bill Holm

COLUMBIA RIVER LADLE, 19th century

Mountain goat horn #1122

A finely carved beaver tops the handle of this ladle, shaped from the long tapering tip of a mountain goat horn. Interlocking negative triangles form rows of zigzags to decorate the flattened underside of the bowl, which may be of upper Chinookan Wasco or Wishxam manufacture.

CHINOOK WOODEN LADLE, Circa 1870

Possibly alder #1092

The pointed ends and animal effigy on the handle are characteristic of Columbia River ladles. Carved of alder or other wood, documented examples of such ladles were collected as early as 1839.

WASCO/WISHXAM SHEEP HORN BOWL, 1850

Bighorn sheep horn #1043

Made by steaming and spreading the horn, these incised bowls are among the most treasured heirlooms of Columbia River Indian people and were traded throughout the Columbia River Gorge and into the Puget Sound area. Wasco and Wishxam carvers from the area of The Dalles excelled at making these bowls long before the arrival of Lewis and Clark.

This 1868 portrait of a Nisqually woman shows her wearing an elaborate dentalium head piece, earrings, and breast plate, all of which would have been valued trade items. The young boy at her side is identified as Master McElroy.

PHOTOGRAPHER UNKNOWN.
(COURTESY BURKE MUSEUM OF NATURAL HISTORY AND CULTURE, SEATTLE: L4233)

NISQUALLY HEAD PIECE AND BRAID TIES, Circa 1870

Dentalium shells, glass trade beads, leather, Chinese coins #1104

SIOUX EARRINGS, 1860s

Dentalium shells, leather #1150

PLATEAU BREASTPLATE, 1870

Dentalium shells, harness leather, glass trade beads, Chinese coins. #1149

Before the introduction of trade beads, women adorned themselves with valuable dentalium shells traded inland from the Coast. The head piece, worn across the forehead, and long braid ties incorporate the much-prized cobalt blue beads, white-hearted red trade beads known as Cornaline d'Aleppo. All of these elaborate ornaments made with dentalium shells demonstrated a family's wealth.

BABY CONTEST

AT THE SPEELYI-MI Arts and Crafts Fair each March on the Yakama reservation, the most cherished exhibits are the entrants in the annual baby contest.

Imagine that you are asked to judge such entries in front of doting mothers, aunts, and grandmothers. Each is convinced that her baby deserves to take first prize. The other two judges are elders who are accustomed to these contests. You worry that you will make a misstep.

But as you study each baby in turn, you share the women's pride and love, and you are happy to be where you are. You admire an infant safely swaddled in an ornate cradleboard, a toddler in a deer hide dress complete with tiny moccasins topped by beaded leggings, a small child with fur strips extending her stubby braids. A miniature war dancer wears a fancy feather bustle. After you have examined all the babies' finery, you and the other judges agree on the winners, the children dressed most traditionally. You thank the mothers for the pleasure of meeting their children, and the contest is over.

PHOTO BY BETTY HEINL, COURTESY OF *TOPPENISH REVIEW*.

CAYUSE CRADLE BOARD, MAYNARD WHITE OWL LAVADOUR, CAYUSE/NEZ PERCE, 1999.

Wood, leather, glass seed beads   #3010

When Maynard White Owl Lavadour's grandmother was four years old, her family lived in an encampment on the Plateau. One day she vanished. The family looked for her for several days and had almost given up hope when she reappeared. "Where have you been?" the family asked.

"I have been away, but the deer took care of me," she told them. Ever since that time, the deer has had special meaning for Lavadour and his family. The image at the top of the cradleboard refers to this legend, and reminds Lavadour of the role the deer played in watching over his family.

This cradleboard is meant for a boy who traditionally would grow up to be a hunter. The red line into the deer from its mouth is the living spirit flowing into the animal. While the artist worked on this cradleboard between January and May of 1999 there were two blue moons, hence the blue moon in this design. The light blue background of the beadwork contains clusters of spirals. Each spiral represents ancestors who are still with us and who are always watching over us, according to Lavadour. (Pamplin 1998)

BABY CONTEST

ARAPAHO BABY'S MOCCASINS WITH LEGGINGS, late 19th century

Hide, glass seed beads #1147

These tiny moccasins with knee-high leggings are from the personal collection of the Reverend H. R. Voth who lived among the Cheyenne and Arapaho from 1882 to 1889. Because of their small size, they may have been made for the missionary as model examples of the style of the time. A tag attached to a legging states: "1889."

PLATEAU CHILD'S DOLL, Circa 1920s

Buckskin, trade cloth, glass seed and larger beads, hide, horsehair, calico, dentalium shells #1131

A wonderful child's companion outfitted with great care in beaded buckskin dress that features the traditional deer tail detail in the beadwork at the neck along with moccasins, panel belt, and a floral-design handbag. Her undergarments are made from calico cloth.

PLATEAU CHILD'S DOLL AND CRADLE BOARD, circa 1880

Wood, trade cloth, buckskin, ribbon, glass seed beads #1136

This large doll, in her elaborately decorated high-back cradle board, would be a prized possession for any little girl. This style of board, when full size, generally was made for dress and could be carried on a horse safely attached to the mother's saddle. The early floral pattern of the beadwork indicates this toy's great age.

PLATEAU WOMAN'S LEGGINGS, 1900–1920

Trade cloth, glass seed beads, velvet, hide #1008

Leggings of this style are part of the finery worn by well-dressed Plateau women on special occasions. They were once owned by a family living at Celilo.

HONORING LIFE'S MILESTONES

TO THIS DAY, THE PEOPLE OF THE COLUMBIA REGION hold feasts in longhouses along the river and across the Plateau to honor the appearance of the first foods of each season—-wild celery, salmon, and roots in the spring, and huckleberries in late summer.

Before each feast, a day is set aside for special ceremonies in the longhouse. Most important are the memorials families hold to end the periods of mourning for dear ones they have lost since the last celebration. This ceremony is necessary before the family can again take part in traditional longhouse activities.

The people recognize other milestones on these occasions or at special ceremonies through the year—a girl's first root digging, a boy's first hunt, the making of a first basket, or the giving of an Indian name. Invited to such a ceremony, you sit on the longhouse bench warmed by the sense of timelessness that the occasion evokes.

Each ceremony includes a "give-away" when all in attendance receive gifts, tokens of remembrance for the day. Gifts are family heirlooms most of us see only in museums, as well as new clothing or household items.

At a memorial, you may see a rare Wasco handbag or a distinctive beaded bag given to a relative or old friend in memory of the loved one. These are objects to be treasured by generation after generation of Native families.

The spirit of honoring elders pervades each event. You sense the family's pride as a young basketmaker solemnly presents her first basket to the woman who taught her to weave. Thus she ensures that the talent will stay with her.

Detail of beaded strap.

WASCO BEADED STRAP, Circa 1850

Trade cloth, hide, sinew, and/or native dogbane fiber threads, and glass seed beads #1062

This strap with the "ancestor" figures similar to those on Wasco twined fiber bags is the only example of its type known. Loom-woven with glass seed beads, straps such as this were worn across the chest to suspend a man's bandolier bag. The stacked triangle motif in the figure's chest is similar to designs used later by Ellen Underwood, whose work appears on p. 50.

D.M.

49

D.M.

WASCO/WISHXAM BEAD-WOVEN BAG, 1850–1870

Trade cloth and glass seed beads #1116

Possibly made by Mumshumsie, the wife of Welawa, head of an Upper Chinook family who lived near present-day Hood River, Oregon. The animal figures with triangular bellies are also found on mid-19th century twined Wasco/Wishxam fiber bags.

G.E.

WASCO/WISHXAM FLAP POUCH, mid-19th century

Dogbane, tule with hide binding #1119

The distinctive motifs on this classic example of Wasco/Wishxam twined basketry represent creatures with which the weavers were familiar in the Columbia Gorge — people, deer or elk, sturgeon and giant condors.

G.E.

WASCO/WISHXAM BEAD-WOVEN POUCH, 1880–1900

Glass seed beads, buckskin #1115

This pouch was probably made by Taswatha (1841-1908), daughter of Upper Chinook Chief Welawa. Later known as Ellen Underwood after her marriage to settler Amos Underwood, she worked distinctive stylized designs into many of these bead-woven bags for both men and women. Her figures relate to those found on traditional twined basketry of her people.

"An Indian man…fell in love with a beautiful Indian girl. She would only come to him at night. One night he decided to follow her and in the morning light he found that she was only a skeleton or bones lying on the ground. The skeleton figure represents bones or death in old Indian stories. In a sense, this means to leave them alone…do not dig them up. Skeleton figures represent that one can enter the spiritual world and re-enter the living world."

"In another old story the frog was in competition with the sun. The frog ended up swallowing the sun and in order to have daylight again, Coyote, the trickster, had to trick the frog into spitting out the sun. The frog's big eyes represent light; closed eyes mean darkness. When the eagle spits lightning it is because our ancestors are angry."

Daryel Lopez

Detail of bandolier bag.

WOVEN BEADWORK BANDOLIER BAG,
Daryel Lopez, Yakama/Nez Perce, 1998
Glass seed beads, bells, feathers, fabric #3006

This loom-woven bandolier bag is made to be worn over the shoulder and across the chest. The beaded patterns tell the story above.

OLD TRADITIONS GREET NEW GENERATIONS **Pat Courtney Gold, Wasco/Wishxam/Tlingit, 1999**

Raffia, jute, suede cloth #3007

This basket is a tribute to the artist's dedication to reviving the almost-forgotten basketry technique of her Wasco/Wishxam people and to preserving their unique figurative designs. Pat Courtney Gold often uses these traditional designs to express contemporary ideas.

NAMEGIVING

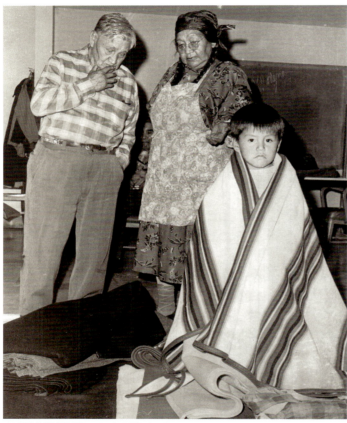

PHOTO BY MARY SCHLICK, COURTESY OF *TOPPENISH REVIEW*.

D.M.

PLATEAU LOOP NECKLACE, 1870–1910

Harness leather, hide, clamshell beads, abalone shell, glass trade beads #1021

By the 1870s, loop necklaces of this design were the most popular style worn by Crow and Plateau men. Usually made of bone disc beads obtained in trade with non-Indians, this example differs in using clamshell disc beads, likely made by Pomo Indians on the central California coast. These beads are highly valued on the Plateau, and usually are found in women's necklaces. The use of these rare and valued beads in a loop necklace would have indicated the wearer's affluence.

YOU SIT WITH OTHERS along the longhouse wall; the benches are full. All eyes are on the center where the young grandson of a Yakama leader stands small and serious as his grandmother begins to pile gifts on his slight frame. Blankets and shawls, articles of clothing, and ceremonial regalia soon cover the child. The grandmother talks quietly to the elder with the microphone. He calls out an ancestor's name. "From today," he says, "this boy will be known by this name."

As the grandmother speaks to the announcer, he calls on friends and relatives of the departed ancestor. Each comes forward to take a gift from the child's shoulders. All, in turn, tell the boy their memories of the one whose name he will carry. They want him to know what he has to live up to. Many acknowledge the child's new name with a gift of money.

This day you have joined with others as witness to an ancient ceremony that validates a child's lineage, sealed by the giving and receiving of gifts.

The keepsakes given during such a ceremony could include necklaces, traditional garments, coiled baskets for special items, and fine twined weaving.

D.M.

YAKAMA MINIATURE SADDLEBAGS, 1900

Corn husk, trade cloth and hide #1142

Native people made miniature examples of many everyday articles. These unique miniature saddlebags are woven in the complex basketry technique of twining with false embroidery, rather than the more common folded embellished rawhide as on the parfleches. The eight-pointed star is a popular motif for flat twined bags of the Plateau, also woven in this technique.

D.M.

PLATEAU TRADE CLOTH CAPOTE, Circa 1880

Trade cloth and glass seed beads #1128

Called capote after the French word for hooded coat, these blanket or trade cloth coats combined the European front opening with the Native seamstresses' square-cut pattern. The white un-dyed selvedge identifies trade cloth. By the mid 19th century, use of the capote had spread across the Great Plains to the Columbia Plateau with the fur trade.

N.W.

COILED UPPER COWLITZ TRUNK WITH LID, 1870

Western red cedar (Thuja plicata), bear grass (Xerophyllum tenax) #1130

The lid on this basket is plaited cedar bark and the body is coiled of split cedar root and covered with imbricated designs in natural and dyed beargrass and the bark of the cedar root. Imbrication is a folding technique in which a flat element, such as beargrass, covers the coiling stitch, which can only be seen on the inside of the basket.

The shape of the basket and the imagery of men on horseback make this container unusual. The Upper Cowlitz people were closely related through language and kinship ties to the Klikitats, who were also makers of fine coiled baskets.

FIRST FOODS FEAST

SUNDAY IS THE DAY for the feast of thanksgiving for the sacred food of each season. After the beautiful songs of the Washaat service are over on the day of the feast, you sit back as the men put up the tables or roll out the tule mats on the floor and young women of the longhouse set them with utensils and plates and bring in the foods of farm and market.

When all is ready, the singers begin a quiet beat on their hand drums, and the ceremonial servers enter laden with foods that have sustained the people of the Plateau since time immemorial, foods of the earth and of the river.

To gather these traditional foods, in each season selected women collect the spring shoots of wild celery or, later, they climb into the hills to dig bitterroot and other food roots. In late summer they go into the mountains to pick berries. The men bring in the first salmon and the deer. After taking part in the seasonal ceremony, all are free to gather the honored foods for their own families.

A feast offers an opportunity to see heirloom baskets in use. Traditionally, the ceremonial root diggers and berry pickers wore brimless basketry hats at these feasts. Seeing such hats in use at the ceremony today reminds you that weavers are reviving this unique Columbia Plateau basket form.

You appreciate the usefulness of the pouch a server wears on her belt, which leaves her hands free to work. The essential digging tool and the soft, round twined root bags also are honored in the sacred rite.

At the end of the summer, berry pickers today pick into strong and mold-resistant cedar root baskets and use them to present the fruits of their labor at the annual huckleberry feast.

PHOTO BY MARSHA SHEWCZYK, COURTESY OF *SPILYAY TYMOO*.

KLIKITAT COILED CEDAR ROOT BASKET, 1890

Western red cedar *(Thuja plicata)*, bear grass *(Xerophyllum tenax)* #1082

Coiling this basket with the split roots of the Western red cedar, the weaver achieved the spectacular "mountain" pattern by a folding technique known as imbrication using the glossy leaves of beargrass and the bark of the cedar root. Native dyes are yellow from Oregon grape root and black from alkaline mud. The twisted bear grass edge that outlines the loops or "ears" required special skill.

These loops allow pickers to lace strings across a layer of foliage to protect the full basket of berries. This three-gallon basket is designed to be carried on the back, supported by a woven strap around the basket and over the forehead, an efficient way to take berries back to camp.

YAKAMA DIGGING STICK AND ROOT GATHERING BAGS, Circa 1920

Iron, wood, cotton string, hide #1084

Although fish and game provided an important part of the Plateau diet at the time of contact with Europeans, the majority of calories that sustained the Native peoples came from the plant foods, many of them roots that grew plentifully on the uplands above the rivers. This iron digging stick, a style that continues in use today, replaced the tool of fire-hardened wood which had been used for centuries for loosening food roots from the soil. By the 20th century, wood was used instead of antler on all but heirloom digger handles.

Round bags twined from strong grasses or dogbane cordage held the roots during digging. Cotton string began to be used for making the bags around the turn of the 20th century. Known by many as "sally" bags, these containers continue to be made and used (when available) for digging roots, for storing other items, and as reminders of the arts of earlier times.

FIRST FOODS FEAST

D.M.

D.M.

PLATEAU BELT WITH POUCH, 20th century

Corn husk, wool yarn, hide, metal buckles #1098

This belt would have been worn horizontally around the waist. This vertical view shows its rich detail. Worked in cornhusk and colored yarns using false embroidery, these stately geometric designs are characteristic of Yakama weaving. The belt pouch provides a safe and convenient carrier for small valuables when the wearer is dressed for a celebration.

PLATEAU TAIL DRESS, 19th century

Deer hide, trade cloth, sinew #1099

This tail dress is constructed of two deer hides with the tail portions folded outward at the shoulders and the tails displayed at the center of the back and front neckline. The edges of the hide have been cut into fringes to form a simple but elegant detail. The belt is described on p. 30

On later beaded dresses, the shape of the tail was commemorated in the beading pattern at the neckline. That custom continues today.

D.M.

HORSES Nettie Jackson, Klikitat/Wasco, 1999.

Recipient, National Heritage Fellowship Award 2000, National Endowment for the Arts.

Western red cedar and beargrass #3008

   Just the size to hold a generous gallon of huckleberries, this basket honors the horse culture. In its materials (the root of the western red cedar and beargrass) and its purpose the basket also honors the great summer gatherings in the Cascade Mountains where Nettie Jackson's people and their neighbors on the Plateau met to pick berries, race their horses, and gather more roots and grass for winter's weaving.

D.M.

PLATEAU WOMAN'S HAT, Circa 1890

Dogbane, beargrass, native dyes #1110

   While among the Nez Perce on their return trip to St. Louis in 1806, Meriwether Lewis noted that the women "wear a cap or cup on the head formed of beargrass and cedarbark." Lewis was correct about beargrass. However, the foundation material was spun dogbane rather than cedar. Worn by women living along the Columbia from Nez Perce country to below the Cascades, these hats usually bore the three-part "mountain design." The brimless twined hats continue to be made today and are seen at most ceremonial and social occasions of the Plateau people.

LONGHOUSE WEDDINGS

YOU ARE INVITED to the marriage ceremony of a young Yakama couple, and you make your way to the Rock Creek Longhouse, nestled in a quiet valley near the north bank of the Columbia River.

Settling into your seat along the longhouse wall, you hear the start of a high, plaintive song. The singers, men holding big wafer-like drums, stand at the front and begin a steady beat.

The father of the bride enters the door at the back of the longhouse, followed by the young couple. The bride wears a white wing dress, her long braids wrapped in furs. To your surprise, on her head is a traditional Plateau-style wedding veil of dentalium shells, beads, and Chinese coins, an adornment rarely seen since the 19th century.

All the bride's attendants, even two small flower girls, wear dresses made of contemporary fabrics in the style of the early deer hide dress. Two of the bridesmaids wear elaborate beaded wedding veils similar to the bride's. The veils, treasured family keepsakes, were brought out for the ceremony by the bridesmaids' Warm Springs grandmother. This is an occasion to remember.

PHOTO BY MARY SCHLICK.

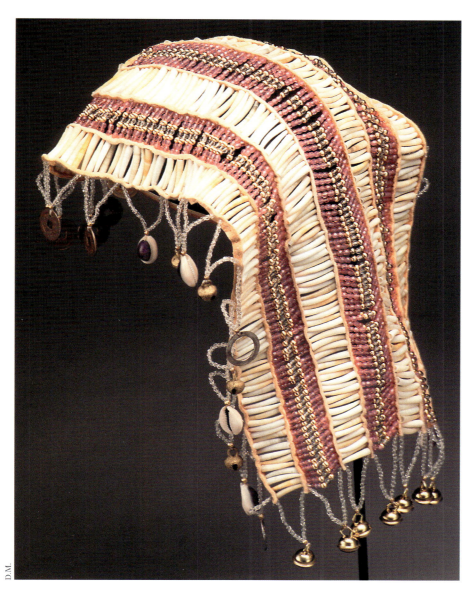

**BRIDAL VEIL Sophie George, Wasco/
Wishxam/Cowlitz/Wenatchi, 1999.
Recipient, National Heritage Fellowship
Award 1998, National Endowment for
the Arts.**

**Dentalium, shells, coins, hide, glass
trade beads, and gold beads #3009**

The materials in this contemporary interpretation of a ceremonial Plateau bride's
headdress represent long tradition, according to the artist. The dentalium shell comes
from the ocean floor and was used for currency long before beads, thimbles, bells and
Chinese coins arrived with the traders. Deer,
elk or bison provided the sinew for thread.

It is tradition that each section of the veil be
sewn with a single long thread to insure
that the couple will always be one.

To illustrate the importance of the veil,
Sophie George's grandmother told her of a
groom's family who brought five of their
best racehorses just to place the veil on the
bride.

LONGHOUSE WEDDINGS

ON THE PLATEAU, the word "wedding" refers to the solemn marriage ceremony before witnesses. It also refers to the lively trades between relatives of the bride and groom. Both are occasions for bringing out prized family heirlooms.

At a wedding trade, you will see families giving keepsakes related to the traditional men's and women's roles. Members of the groom's family bring items made or purchased by men to exchange with the bride's relatives for items made or gathered by women. A woman's beaded bag could be traded for a carved wooden mortar if their values were agreed upon as equal. Her twined storage bag filled with dried roots might be exchanged for a parfleche, an "Indian suitcase," packed with shawls and scarves. An old custom during such trading was for a groom's relative to place a stick on the longhouse floor to represent a horse that waited outside, to be traded for something equally valuable.

WISHXAM OAK BURL BOWL, 19th century

#1044

These graceful mortars were family treasures used for pulverizing berries, fish, and roots with a basalt pestle. According to the artist Nettie Jackson, the village carver who made such bowls from the knots of oak trees was highly respected for his skills, (Pamplin, 1998)

NEZ PERCE BEADED BAGS, 1890–1900

Glass seed beads and hide #1046

Contour beaded floral designs are found across the Plateau. By following the contour of the design when applying the background beads, the makers created a distinctive three-dimensional effect. The smaller of these bags may have been made for a man's dress use. Contour beading technique was largely discontinued in the 1920s. Artists such as Maynard White Owl Lavadour, Sophie George and others are revitalizing the technique.

UMATILLA PARFLECHE, Circa 1850

Buffalo rawhide #1139c

Fully incised rawhide containers are extremely rare. The buffalo hide of this parfleche from the Umatilla, Oregon, area has been darkened with blood to increase the contrast in the pattern. The incised decorative motifs are nearly identical to those on the matched Sioux pair below. Much prized today, these often are referred to as "Indian trunks" or "suitcases" on the Plateau. This parfleche was featured in *The American Indian Parfleche: A Tradition of Abstract Painting* by Gaylord Torrence, as was one of a matched pair of Sioux parfleches (below).

PLATEAU STORAGE BAG, Circa 1860

Cornhusk or native grass, dogbane. #1132

The beauty of these early storage bags, made before commercial wool or dyes were introduced on the Plateau, lies in the warm tones of the natural spun dogbane background and the native grass or cornhusk false embroidery. The maker of this bag followed the Plateau tradition of using a different design on each side.

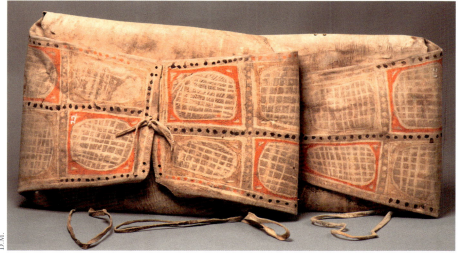

SIOUX PARFLECHES, 1850–60

Buffalo hide, ochre, and other pigments #1139a, b

This matched pair of Sioux buffalo rawhide carrying cases is decorated with native red and yellow ochre and black pigments. The crosshatch pattern was created by scraping through the surface to expose a lighter layer. Known as "parfleches" (from the French Canadian for "to parry arrows") such cases frequently were made in pairs and can be seen in historic photos hanging from a pack saddle on each side of a horse. A portion of hide has been cut from the flap of one of these cases, perhaps to mend a moccasin sole.

THE EARLIEST RECORDS OF THE PEOPLE of the Columbia Plateau are found in the legends passed down through generations by the elders, and in the ancient images that watch from the rocks along the rivers. These stories tell of the time before time, of the days when the animals were people.

Wasco/Yakama artist Lillian Pitt carries on the story-telling tradition in her masks and other works in clay and bronze. These are modern versions of the history recorded on painted hides and in the ledger book drawings of the artists of the Plains.

COYOTE SPIRIT, **Lillian Pitt, Wasco/Yakama, 1998. Recipient of the Oregon Governor's Arts Award 1990**

Cast bronze #3000

Contemporary artist Lillian Pitt has named this mask for the Coyote character that appears in stories shared among American Indian families. Her work as a ceramic artist and sculptor grows from her desire to preserve images and stories told by the first residents of the Columbia River Gorge.

Coyote is the legendary trickster. Often he is the victim of his own buffoonery and plots. Many Columbia River tribes consider him responsible for creation, death, and rules of conduct. He sets an example of what not to be. Coyote, the animal, is as wily and inventive as his persona in the stories.

"Many years ago, when people and animals communicated easily, Coyote came down the gorge and met Tsagigla'lal, a capable woman who led her people. 'Changes are coming,' Coyote warned Tsagigla'lal. 'How will you watch over your people when changes arrive?'

'I don't know,' Tsagigla'lal replied. To help her, Coyote changed her into a rock to watch over her people from the Columbia Gorge wall."

Lillian Pitt

D.M.

SHE WHO WATCHES Lillian Pitt, Wasco/Yakama, 1998

Cast bronze #3005

This representation of the woman chief, Tsagigla'lal or She Who Watches, is found among the pictographs and petroglyphs along the basalt cliffs of the Columbia River Gorge. The image has protective and nurturing associations for the artist whose aim is to create a consciousness of the need for healing and a sense of the transformative magic in ordinary things and beings.

SOURCES

Afton, Jean, David Fridtjof Halaas, Andrew E. Masich, with Richard N. Ellis. *Cheyenne Dog Soldiers: A Ledgerbook History of Coups and Combat*. Niwot and Denver: University Press of Colorado and the Colorado Historical Society, 1997.

Albright, Peggy. *Crow Indian Photographer: The Work of Richard Throssel*. Albuquerque: University of New Mexico Press, 1997.

Cowdrey, Mike. *Arrow's Elk Society Ledger: A Southern Cheyenne Record of the 1870's*. Santa Fe, New Mexico: Morning Star Gallery, 1999.

Coues, Elliott. "List of Property forwarded from Fort George for the Upper Country, Jan. 3d, 1814. " In The *Manuscript Journals of Alexander Henry and of David Thompson, 1799-1814,* Vol. II, pp. 822-23. Ross & Haines, Inc., Minneapolis. 1897.

Dodge, Colonel Richard Irving. *Our Wild Indians: Thirty-three Years' Personal Experience Among the Red Men of the Great West*. Hartford, CT. : Worthington and Co., 1882. Reissued in 1959, New York: Archer House Inc.

Duncan, Kate C. *Northern Athapaskan Art: A Beadwork Tradition*. Seattle: University of Washington Press, 1989.

Ewers, John Canfield, "Saddles of the Plains Indians," in *Man Made Mobile: Early Saddles of Western North America*, edited by Richard E. Ahlborn, pages 72-84. Washington, D.C.: Smithsonian Institution Press, 1980.

Grafe, Steven L. "'Our Private Affairs in Way of Barter': Correspondence between Dudley Allen and Henry Harmon Spalding, 1838-1848" in *Idaho Yesterdays*, Volume 40, Number 3, Fall 1996, pp. 2-12.

Howell, Darrel S. *Reflections: The Darrel S. Howell Collection*. Stockton, California. Bradley Printing, 1995.

Hunn, Eugene, with James Selam and Family, *Nch'i wána, "The Big River": Mid-Columbia Indians and their Land*. Seattle: University of Washington Press, 1990.

Hyde, George E. *Life of George Bent Written from His Letters*. Norman: University of Oklahoma Press, 1968.

Lewis, Meriwether and William Clark. *The Journals of Lewis and Clark*, ed. by Gary Moulton. Volume 7. Lincoln: University of Nebraska Press, 1991.

Lincoln, Louise. *Southwest Indian Silver from the Doneghy Collection*. Minneapolis, Minnesota: Minneapolis Institute of Arts and the University of Texas, Austin, 1982.

Lowie, Robert H. "Crow Indian Art," *Anthropological Papers of the American Museum of Natural History* XXI (IV): 273-322, 1922.

Ludwickson, John, and John M. O'Shea. *Archaeology and Ethnohistory of the Omaha Indians: The Big Village Site*. (Studies in Anthropology of North American Indians). Lincoln: University of Nebraska Press, 1990.

Marquis, Thomas B., Interpreter. *Wooden Leg: A Warrior Who Fought Custer*. Minneapolis: The Midwest Company, 1932. (Reprint edition, Lincoln and London: University of Nebraska Press, 1964.)

Maryhill Museum of Art, "A Gathering: American Indian Art from the Pamplin Collection." Goldendale, WA, Maryhill Museum. 1999.

Mooney, James *The Ghost Dance Religion and Sioux Outbreak of 1890*. Fourteenth Annual Report of the Bureau of American Ethnology, 1892-93. Part 2. Washington, D.C., 1896.

Orchard, William C. *The Technique of Porcupine Quill Decoration Among The North American Indians*. New York: The Museum of The American Indian Heye Foundation. La Salle Litho Corporation., 1971.

Pamplin, Dr. Robert B. Jr., *The Pamplin Collection of American Indian Art*. Video created by Bonnie B. Kahn and Gary Eisler. Interviews with Sophie George, Bill Holm, Nettie Jackson, Maynard White Owl Lavadour, Daryel Lopez, Lillian Pitt, and Mary Schlick. Portland, Oregon, 1998.

Ramsey, Jarold, *Coyote Was Going There*, Seattle: University of Washington Press, 1977.

Riggs, Thomas L., *Sunset to Sunset: A Lifetime with My Brothers the Dakotas*. South Dakota State Historical Society Press, 1958.

Ross, Lester A. "Glass Beads, in Fort Vancouver 1829-1860," pp. 628-770. National Park Service, Mss. on file Fort Vancouver National Historic Site, Vancouver, Washington., 1976.

Schlick, Mary Dodds. *Columbia River Basketry: Gift of the Ancestors, Gift of the Earth*. Seattle and London: University of Washington Press, 1994.

Stearns, Robert E. C. "Ethno Conchyology: A Study of Primitive Money." Pp. 297-334 in *Report of the U. S. National Museum Under the Direction of the Smithsonian Institution for 1886-87*. Washington: U. S. Government Printing Office, 1889.

Steffen, Randy. *The Horse Soldier 1776-1943: The United States Cavalryman: His Uniforms, Arms, Accouterments, and Equipments*. Vol. I *The Revolution, the War of 1812, the Early Frontier, 1776-1850*. Norman: University of Oklahoma Press, 1977.

———— Vol. II *The Frontier, the Mexican War, the Civil War, the Indian Wars 1851-1880*. Norman: University of Oklahoma Press, 1978.

———— Vol. III *The Last of the Indian Wars, The Spanish-American War, The Brink of the Great War 1881-1916*. Norman: University of Oklahoma Press, 1978.

Taylor, Colin, ed. *The Native Americans, the Indigenous People of North America*. New York: Smithmark, 1991.

Taylor, Colin F., *The Plains Indians: A Cultural and Historic View of the North American Plains Tribes of the Pre Reservation Period*. Avenel, New Jersey: Salamander Books, 1994.

Thom, Laine and C.J. Brafford. *Dancing Colors: Paths of Native American Women*. Vancouver, British Columbia: Raincoast Books, 1992.

Viola, Herman J. *Little Bighorn Remembered: The Untold Indian Story of Custer's Last Stand*. New York: Times Books, a division of Random House, 1999.

Woodward, Arthur. *Indian Trade Goods*. Portland: Oregon Archaeological Society, 1965.

Dr. Robert B. Pamplin, Jr. is a businessman, philanthropist, farmer, minister, and author of 13 books. His wife, Marilyn, is involved with volunteer organizations and many philanthropic boards, and has been recognized for her dedication to children's issues. Touching lives is the Pamplins' mission. Preserving and sharing American Indian cultures and art is an important part of that legacy.

The Oregon Historical Society presented the exhibition, *Keeping the Spirit Alive*, at the Oregon History Center in Portland, Oregon, February through November 2001. *Keeping the Spirit Alive*, the exhibition and catalog, were made possible through the generosity of Dr. & Mrs. Robert B. Pamplin, Jr.

ACKNOWLEDGEMENTS

THE AUTHORS WOULD LIKE TO ACKNOWLEDGE the following people for their assistance with the exhibition and the catalog: Francine Havercroft and Colleen Schafroth of Maryhill Museum of Art in Goldendale, Washington for their assistance and ideas from earlier exhibitions of this collection; Cultural Ethnologist Craig D. Bates for his editorial suggestions; Cultural Resource Specialist Chuck Hibbs, and retired U.S. Customs Agent and metallurgist Harvey Steele for their comments on early drafts of the manuscript. Thanks also to the hard working men and women of the Multnomah County Library Reference Desk.

Thanks also go to the Artist Maynard White Owl Lavadour, for his suggestions with regard to display of the collection. Special thanks to Kenneth Edgar Kahn, Jr. and to Anne Elizabeth Kahn for their patience

We would like to thank the following men and women of the Oregon Historical Society for the talents they brought to the production and creation of the exhibition and catalog. Richard Jost for the fine work he did in scanning the artwork and photographs. Adair Law for her shepherding of the catalog, Marsha Matthews for keeping all the pieces moving forward and thanks to Chet Orloff for saying yes to the idea. We also thank Karen Kirtley for her editorial skill and patience.

COLOPHON

THE TYPEFACES USED IN *Keeping the Spirit Alive* are Engraver's Gothic and Arbitrary on the cover, Fairfield and Humanist for the interior.

Book Design	J & B Creative
Cover Design	Champlin Design Group
Printing	Bridgetown Printing Co.
Photography	Gary Eisler, Dennis Maxwell, Nayland Wilkins

ABOUT THE AUTHORS

BONNIE KAHN began working on the Pamplin Collection of American Indian Art several years ago. She has twenty years of experience in working closely with Native American artists, helping them to develop and market their art work. With the support of Dr. and Mrs. Robert B. Pamplin, Jr., Ms. Kahn has shaped the Pamplin Collection of American Indian Art so that it focuses on the Horse Cultures of the Plateau and Plains. Dr. Pamplin's initial interest was in dramatic artifacts connected with warrior culture of the Plains and Plateau. Realizing that the warrior culture did not exist in a vacuum but was interdependent on all members of the group, his interests broadened to include work that covered family and domestic life. With Ms. Kahn's expertise and assistance, Dr. Pamplin collects actively.

The Pamplin Collection contains fine examples of historical and contemporary work. As a collector, Dr. Pamplin looks for work of exceptional quality and rarity. When a piece is being considered for the Pamplin Collection, a systematic analysis is done. The work is analyzed by cultural resource consultants, tribal members and ethnologists, as well as experts in identifying forgeries. Microanalysis, ultraviolet analysis, and radiographs are some of the methods used to correctly identify the components of various pieces. After all analysis is completed, the item is then accepted as part of the collection.

The Pamplin Collection continues to grow and includes contemporary work as well. The contemporary work tends to have strong roots in the past at the same time it pushes forward into new media and artistic areas. It is work that continues to keep the spirit alive.

MARY SCHLICK'S first view of the Pamplin Collection surprised her with memories.

The extraordinary objects in the collection were much more than works of art to her. She had seen their counterparts in use by Native families over the years and realized that they continue to be part of a rich and ancient heritage whose spirit is vibrantly alive among the people of the Columbia Plateau today.

She came to the Colville reservation in north central Washington in 1950 with her husband, William, who was beginning his career as a forester with the Bureau of Indian Affairs. Young strangers from the Midwest, the couple was quietly taken into the lives of the Colville people. Later, the family lived on the Warm Springs, then the Yakama reservation where William Schlick served as reservation superintendent. Upon his retirement from federal service in 1978, they settled in the upper Hood River Valley and continued their close association with the Native people of the Columbia Plateau.

Active in community life, Ms. Schlick helped start a cooperative kindergarten at Warm Springs that soon became the first tribal HeadStart program in the country, and, with Yakama educators, developed a model culture-based preschool curriculum. Studying the distinctive basketry of the region with elders and in museum collections, she wrote *Columbia River Basketry, Gift of the Ancestors, Gift of the Earth,* (University of Washington Press, 1994) after moving to Oregon's Hood River Valley. A basket-maker herself, she was awarded an Oregon Governor's Arts Award in 1998 for her advocacy of Native artists. Ms. Schlick now serves as adjunct curator for the Native American collection at Maryhill Museum. She has curated exhibits of Native arts for many northwest museums including the Oregon History Center.